Outside the Walls

Outside the Walls

Encountering God in the Unfamiliar

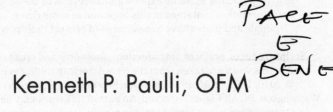

Pat and Jim —

Peace & Beng!

Kenneth P. Paulli, OFM

Father Paulli

WESTBOW
PRESS®
A DIVISION OF THOMAS NELSON
& ZONDERVAN

Easter 2018

WestBow Press books may be ordered through booksellers or by contacting:

WestBow Press
A Division of Thomas Nelson & Zondervan
1663 Liberty Drive
Bloomington, IN 47403
www.westbowpress.com
1 (866) 928-1240

Because of the dynamic nature of the Internet, any web addresses or links contained in this book may have changed since publication and may no longer be valid. The views expressed in this work are solely those of the author and do not necessarily reflect the views of the publisher, and the publisher hereby disclaims any responsibility for them.

This book is a work of non-fiction. Unless otherwise noted, the author and the publisher make no explicit guarantees as to the accuracy of the information contained in this book and in some cases, names of people and places have been altered to protect their privacy.

Scripture texts, prefaces, introductions, footnotes and cross references used in this work are taken from the New American Bible, revised edition © 2010, 1991, 1986, 1970 Confraternity of Christian Doctrine, Inc., Washington, DC All Rights Reserved. No part of this work may be reproduced or transmitted in any form or by any means, electronic or mechanical, including photocopying, recording, or by any information storage and retrieval system, without permission in writing from the copyright owner.

Any people depicted in stock imagery provided by Thinkstock are models, and such images are being used for illustrative purposes only. Certain stock imagery © Thinkstock.

ISBN: 978-1-9736-1429-6 (sc)
ISBN: 978-1-9736-1430-2 (hc)
ISBN: 978-1-9736-1428-9 (e)

Library of Congress Control Number: 2018900319

Print information available on the last page.

WestBow Press rev. date: 02/14/2018

Dedication

A miei carissimi genitori,

Maria Luisa e Paolo Giacomo (defunto)

Contents

Contents

Foreword

It was the Solemnity of All the Saints 1978 when I first met Ken Paulli. He was an undergraduate student at the University of New York at Albany's campus. I remember the moment: it was the evening celebration of the feast, and he was in the Communion procession on my side of the aisle. As he approached the head of the line, he reverently bowed, and I immediately sensed something most unique about this young person. I shared with him the Body of Christ. We have been in a communion of friendship ever since. Amen!

Through these nearly forty years, I have known Ken as: a pupil, a mentee, an undergraduate student, a graduate student, a doctoral student, a young Franciscan in formation, a newly ordained parish priest, a college professor, a college administrator, a parish mission preacher, and, now, as a published author. Therefore, it is with great gratitude that I write this foreword to his first of what I am sure will be several books of this genre.

Outside the Walls is an autobiographical memoir of sorts, a record of his spiritual journey into the mystery of Christ. Each chapter of this book is inspired by the founder of the Franciscan Order, Saint Francis of Assisi. From this inspiration, Fr. Ken, a member of the Order of Friars Minor, shares a personal story of encountering God through the most unlikely encounters with others. Moreover, in an effort to understand what God is asking of him through these human/divine encounters, he draws upon his Franciscan tradition, as well as the Roman Catholic tradition, to make sense of the mystery that is unfolding as a gift into his heart. In all the ways by which I have known Fr. Ken, through these two score years, this book, I believe, captures the essence of what I saw in him long ago. He shows himself in this writing to be a person well aware of his gifts. At the same time, he willingly acknowledges his brokenness and prays at the end of each chapter for divine assistance and a strengthening of faith, hope, and love. All of this is written and offered in service to others, who find themselves on their own journey of faith. He writes in a personal way to invite those who read this book to do the same: to understand the subtle and lovely presence of God in the most unexpected people and places. In other words, to be open to surprise! This is Fr. Ken at his best!

Personally, this book worked just as Fr. Ken intended it to for me and any other reader. As I read his stories, I was led to examine my own experiences of God in the unexpected moments of life. One particular incident came vividly to mind as I read Fr. Ken's account of the woman who simply wanted love from her visitors. As I read this chapter, I remembered my own paternal grandmother, Catherine, once saying to me, as I was visiting her: "Please, don't abandon me!" And then she added: "When you visit me, I know that God has not abandoned me!" It hit me then and there the truth that we proclaim as Catholics about the Incarnation of God. We profess that God comes to us, through us. My dear grandmother was alerting me that, in our pain and aloneness, in our vulnerability and fear, we are the living icons of the presence of Christ to each other. I knew the doctrine, but I did not yet feel the doctrine and experience it in the heart until I heard her speak quite unexpectedly from her own pain. May this book do the same for all those who have the joy of reading it. So, thank you, Fr. Ken, for the time and energy you have given to bring this book to print. You are like the wise and elegant steward of the Gospels, who could bring from his storehouse both the old and the new. I look forward to your next endeavor, as I chuckle to myself: the pupil has become the teacher!

Rev. Richard N. Fragomeni, PhD
Catholic Theological Union
The Feast of Saint James, Apostle
25 July 2017

Acknowledgments

No book gets to print without the assistance of many. On the occasion of my first published book, I want to acknowledge some of the many who were involved in *Outside the Walls*.

I am grateful to my Province, Holy Name, for supporting my spiritual and intellectual journey. In particular, I am grateful to Fr. Peter Fiore, OFM, a longtime friend and mentor, for encouraging me as a writer and for his publishing experience and expertise.

I am grateful to my mother, Maria Luisa, not only for her life of Christian discipleship, but also for the hours she spent proofreading this manuscript.

I am grateful to James Garbaini for his Microsoft Word expertise and for his assistance with this manuscript.

I am grateful to Fr. Richard N. Fragomeni, another longtime friend and mentor, for writing the foreword.

I am grateful to Alan Colavecchio, a dear friend, for designing the cover.

ONE

ONE

Francis and the Walls of Assisi

In his first encyclical, *Evangelii Gaudium*, *The Joy of the Gospel*, invoking the Pauline principle that authentic Christian communities are those that never forget the poor, Pope Francis writes,

> This is why I want a Church which is poor and for the poor. They have so much to teach us ... We need to let ourselves be evangelized by them ... We are called to find Christ in them, to lend our voices to their causes, but also to be their friends, to listen to them, to speak for them and to embrace the mysterious wisdom which God wishes to share with us through them. (par. 198)

The poor are our friends. The poor are our teachers. The poor reveal the suffering Christ in ways others cannot. We are called, says Pope Francis, far beyond involving ourselves in a few sporadic acts of generosity on behalf of the poor to stay close to the poor as we become new creations in Christ. (par. 188)

Francis of Assisi, the great thirteenth-century saint from the beautiful Umbrian hill town of Assisi, knew how important it was to "stay close to the poor" long before Pope Francis penned the above words, and specifically to lepers. As the son of Lady Pica and Pietro Bernardone, a wealthy cloth merchant, the early years of Francis's life—a life lived within the walled city of Assisi—were for Francis most comfortable. As a family within the newly emerging merchant class of thirteenth-century Europe, Francis enjoyed safety, good food and drink, friends, guaranteed future employment in the family business, respect, and power.

Not particularly interested in the cloth business, however, and having failed miserably at serving the people of Assisi as a knight when Assisi was at war with Perugia, Francis began to hear and discern that God had something else in mind for how Francis would serve his fellow Assisians, the church, and the larger world. Curiously, Francis was only able to hear and discern God's plan for him when he left the known, familiar, safe, and secure walled city of Assisi and lived outside the walls, where so much for Francis was unknown, unfamiliar, and, frankly, scary.

While outside the walls, Francis encountered what previously he never ever would have wanted to encounter— lepers. Thomas of Celano, Francis's first biographer, describes the encounter with these words:

> Then the holy lover of profound humility moved to the lepers and stayed with them. For God's sake he served all of them with great love. He washed the filth from them, and even cleaned out the puss from their sores, just as he said in his testament: "When I was in sin, it seemed too bitter for me to see lepers, and the Lord led me among them and I showed mercy to them." For he used to say that the sight of the lepers was so bitter to him that in the days of his vanity when he saw their houses even two miles away, he would cover his nose with his hand. (*First Life of Saint Francis*, par. 17)

Led by the Lord, according to Francis himself, and led outside the walls of his hometown, Francis encountered lepers. He served them. He touched them. He cleaned their sores. He stayed with them. Why? Because Francis above all else wanted to love the Lord, who willingly suffered for our sake. Outside the walls and led by the Lord, the suffering Christ was revealed to Francis in and through the suffering lepers in ways no other human beings could do for Francis. That is why Francis continued to stay among lepers and insisted that those who wanted to join his way of life do the same. You see, outside the walls Francis learned that certainly there were things he could do to serve lepers—for example, to help them clean their sores. More importantly, however, Francis learned that he needed lepers more than they needed him. Why? Because despite whatever service he might offer to them, they revealed the face of the suffering Christ to him in ways no other could. In the words of Pope Francis, Francis learned from them "the mysterious wisdom which God wishes to share with us through them."

As a Franciscan friar for more than thirty years, and as a Franciscan priest for more than twenty-five years, I have always been inspired by this notion of living "outside the walls" and "staying with lepers"; at the same time, it has also been a challenging dimension to Franciscan life for me. Even more than a life of radical poverty, and even more than a life lived alone in caves and in deep contemplative prayer, Francis's affirmation to being led outside the walls of Assisi to encounter that which he for so long had found bitter—so that he could encounter the sweetness of the suffering Christ in lepers—is the legacy that most moves me each day to do my best to walk this way of life. Though really difficult, I too have come to learn that saying yes to the Lord's lead in my life often means going outside the walls of my usual comfortable home and town to encounter what I often incorrectly think will be bitter in my life—but that actually turns out to be sweet in the sense that I come to know others, though different from me, as brother and sister. I come to know them in this way precisely because they are able to reveal to me the suffering Christ in ways others cannot.

This book, one I have desired to write and publish for several years, is born primarily from these "outside the walls" encounters I have had over the more than five decades of life I have lived on planet Earth. More specifically, it brings together material I have taught at Siena College in a seminar I have taught many times now—Franciscan service—as well as material I put together for more than twenty years of giving Lenten parish missions across the United States and Canada. I hope you will find the chapters real, inspiring, and helpful. Though they are numbered one through ten, in fact, they can be read in any order. The format for each chapter is the same. Each chapter begins with me, the author, sharing with you, the reader, an "outside the walls" experience in my life—an experience that ultimately got me to ask the question, *Okay, God, what are you asking of me?* This story is then followed by looking to some of the giants who have gone before us and are marked with the sign of faith—people such as St. Peter, Mary of Magdala, and St. Francis of Assisi. I look to them in terms of how they can be so helpful in responding to the earlier question, "Okay, God, what are you asking of me?" Each chapter then concludes with a prayer, questions, and possible action steps for you, the reader, to consider. Read well. Moreover, live well.

TWO

TWO

No, I Am Not the Pope

Maria Teresa, the mother of one of my dear friends, Annie, died in the fall of 2016. She was ninety-eight years old, just three months shy of celebrating her ninety-ninth birthday. For many years prior to her death, Maria Teresa suffered with Alzheimer's disease. For the last seven years of her life, she lived at the Eddy Heritage House Nursing and Rehabilitation Center; it is a 122-bed skilled nursing care center located in Troy, New York. Annie visited her mom nearly every day. When I would see Annie, often she would share with me how difficult it was for her to visit her mom, since the visits when her mom did not recognize her were becoming more and more frequent. Annie's husband caught my ear one day and asked, "Why doesn't God take my mother-in-law? This is no way for her to live. This is no way for Annie to live."

Two years prior to her death, I, along with Annie, went to Troy to visit her mom. In the interest of full disclosure, I do not do well in nursing homes, even as a visitor. I find it so sad to see so many, in one residence, who are unwell and nearing death. Perhaps my discomfort has something to do with seeing what could well be my future. Nevertheless, on that spring morning, Annie and I entered the Eddy Heritage House. Annie signed us in at the front desk, and we made our way down the stairs to a first-floor community room. Almost all of the residents there were in wheelchairs, many of whom were hunched over and asleep, including Maria Teresa, Annie's mom.

Maneuvering our way through the wheelchairs and their occupants, we finally made our way to Annie's mom. Annie stood on her right. I stood on her left. Her eyes were closed, and she appeared to be sleeping. Annie bent over and whispered into her mother's ear, "Ma. Ma. Hi. It's Annie." No response. "Ma," she continued, "it's Annie, and I am here with a priest." Though we both could see and hear that she was breathing, Maria Teresa still gave no response. Finally, Annie spoke a bit more loudly into her mother's ear, saying, "Ma. Friar Paulli is here with me to see you. He is a Franciscan priest, and he is a professor and a vice president at Siena College." No sooner did Annie finish her sentence when her mom opened her eyes, raised her head, and, using rather *colorful language*, shouted for all in the community room to hear that she did not care about any of my titles: college professor, vice president, or priest. In fact, she said, that she didn't care if I were the pope! What she did care about was knowing that I was there to "give her some love." As Maria Teresa put it boldly and powerfully, "If he's not here *to give me some love*, then tell him to go away!" Once I got past the word choice of Annie's mom, a nearly one-hundred-year-old woman, I chuckled to myself and thought, *She's right. If I am not here to give or share some love, then I should not have come.*

In my meditation that night, I thanked God for bringing me to Maria Teresa. My gratitude had little to do with what good I may have done for her, or even for Annie that day. Rather, my gratitude was twofold: first, even a nearly one-hundred-year-old Alzheimer's patient is able to live one's baptismal calling. In other words, the love that the Father freely shares with us in Christ is the very same love that we, the baptized, are called to share with others, especially the sick and dying.

Second, I thought about Annie and her daily commitment to visit her mom, even on the days when her mom had no idea who she was. This is living the faith. This is walking in the footsteps of Jesus. This is what it means to upbuild God's kingdom.

Except for very few people, no one knew, and even to this day, very few people know what Annie daily did for her mom. There were no television cameras at the nursing home. There were no reporters. Annie did not take selfies of herself and send them to the larger world for all to see.

She did not get onto Facebook, Twitter, Instagram, Tumblr, Snapchat, Vine, or Flickr to tell the social media world: "See what good deeds I do each and every day of my life." No. Annie, pained by her mother's deteriorating health, shared love in a rather beautiful and quiet way. Think about it. Is that not the way most of us live our lives as brothers and sisters to the Lord—quietly and humbly, in ways hardly noticed by others?

Annie's quiet, humble, gentle, daily love for her mom reminded me of Jesus's powerful show of love for his disciples in John's gospel:

> Before the feast of Passover, Jesus knew that his hour had come to pass from this world to the Father. He loved his own in the world and he loved them to the end. The devil had already induced Judas, son of Simon the Iscariot, to hand him over. So, during supper, fully aware that the Father had put everything into his power and that he had come from God and was returning to God, he rose from supper and took off his outer garments. He took a towel and tied it around his waist. Then he poured water into a basin and began to wash the disciples' feet and dry them with the towel around his waist. He came to Simon Peter, who said to him, "Master, are you

going to wash my feet?" Jesus answered and said to him, "What I am doing, you do not understand now, but you will understand later." Peter said to him, "You will never wash my feet." Jesus answered him, "Unless I wash you, you will have no inheritance with me." Simon Peter said to him, "Master, then not only my feet, but my hands and head as well." Jesus said to him, "Whoever has bathed has no need except to have his feet washed, for he is clean all over; so you are clean, but not all." For he knew who would betray him; for this reason, he said, "Not all of you are clean." So when he had washed their feet [and] put his garments back on and reclined at table again, he said to them, "Do you realize what I have done for you? You call me 'teacher' and 'master,' and rightly so, for indeed I am. If I, therefore, the master and teacher, have washed your feet, you ought to wash one another's feet. I have given you a model to follow, so that as I have done for you, you should also do. (JN 13:1–15)

Questions:

What about you?

Do you humble yourself to allow Jesus to wash your feet?

Who are the people in your life to whom you need "to show some love," as Maria Teresa put it so candidly?

What do you need to ask from God so that, indeed, you do show that love?

Prayer:

Holy Spirit, breath of God, I pray once more that you breathe in me and show me some love for I am desperate for you, dear Spirit. I know that without your love, I cannot show love to those around me, especially the sick and dying. Help me to understand that you come to us, through us, and that as you breathe in me, so too may I breathe into others the same love that is God. Help me to imagine a world where we all breathe the same breath. Amen.

THREE

THREE

The Buffalo Chip Saloon

In the spring of 2010, a good friend of mine, Brian, a Notre Dame and Michigan Law School grad, said to me, "Hey, the next time you are in the Phoenix area, you must go to the Buffalo Chip Saloon in Cave Creek, Arizona."

"What?" I said.

He replied, "I am serious. Take a look at this piece I just read in the *New York Times*, entitled 'Old and New Wests Meet in Arizona Desert Foothills,' by Elizabeth Maker (May 20, 2010)."

I read the six-page article. For me, the following are the most memorable lines penned by Elizabeth Maker: "Larry Wendt, owner of the Buffalo Chip Saloon & Steakhouse in Cave Creek, explained: 'The state of Arizona has the toughest DUI laws in the country. We've even got RUI laws for riding horses under the influence.'"

Riding [horses] under the influence? I have never heard of such a thing. What must life be like in Cave Creek, Arizona, if such a law is necessary? Maker goes on in the article and writes: "The Buffalo Chip is especially packed on Wednesdays and Fridays, when it offers free bull-riding shows out back. People of all ages watch the bucking broncos and feast on pulled pork from huge smoking barbecue pits. Inside, there are peanuts on the floor, cowboy boots hanging from the ceiling and almost always a live band."

To my friend, I said, "You must be kidding, Brian. I would not be caught dead in such a place!"

Fast forward a few years, to the spring of 2015, on a Friday night, after a round of golf at the Boulders in Carefree,

Arizona, I, and my friends Thomas and Annmarie went to the Buffalo Chip Saloon for dinner and to experience what I had never experienced before, a bull-riding show. Having read the Maker article, I was not surprised to discover peanut shells all over the floor. However, I was surprised by how packed the place was. I was even more surprised by the scores of men and women carrying or wearing firearms!

In terms of dinner, I did not "feast on pulled pork from huge smoking barbecue pits," as described by Maker, but rather, I had the "Three Quarter Pound Choice Ribeye with Cowboy Beans and Biscuit," and a cold beer. The dinner was delicious! Following dinner, my friends and I made our way to the back of what once was a feed and bait shop on the way to Bartlett and Horseshoe Lakes. That is to say, we made our way to the back of the Buffalo Chip Saloon, which is now a two thousand seat bull-riding arena. It was a beautiful, star-filled night and the arena was jammed. Eventually, we found good seats about halfway up the arena. We sat behind what appeared to me to be a "normal," thirty-something mom with two of her kids, one to her left and one to her right.

This particular bull riding contest had three rounds. The first round involved all adult male riders riding larger bulls. The second round involved all younger adult males riding calves. The third, and final round, involved young boys *and* young girls riding sheep. In rounds one and two, emerging from the "bucking chute," the riders attempted to stay on their respective bulls for at least eight seconds, while only touching the bull with their riding hand. In these rounds, the bulls were particularly feisty—rearing, kicking, spinning, and twisting—such that only two riders were able to ride for eight or more seconds. In the third round, however, in order to score any points, young riders needed to ride for only three seconds.

Remember the thirty-something mom in front of me? Well, as round three got under way, she turned around to tell me and my friends that her six-year-old son was competing in this round.

"Six?" I asked.

"Yes ... we like to start riders real young around here," she responded.

I was dumbfounded. Okay. I get it that sheep-riding is less dangerous than bull-riding. However, let us be serious; even riding a sheep, especially as a child, is dangerous. Think about the potential risk for head injuries!

When it was time for her son, whose name is "J. W." (as we would soon learn), to come out of the bucking chute, this normal, thirty-something mom, with a thirty-two ounce mug of beer in one hand, stood up and shouted at the top of her lungs, "J. W.—ride that sheep and kick some butt! Go boy! Go! Go boy! Go!" I was speechless. Part of me thought all of this was quite amusing. Part of me was scared, especially for the young riders. Most of me, however, felt so out-of-place. I knew that being more than twenty-five hundred miles away from my home in New York was not the source of why I felt out-of-place. After all, I was with friends. However, I could not figure out what was the source. Was it the mom in front of me who, at first, seemed like me, and later seemed quite unlike me? Was it that I was among the few not wearing a Stetson hat, or Tony Lama boots, or a Nocana silver buckle on my belt? Was it that I was in a crowd of two thousand people, the majority of whom were carrying firearms? Was it the bull-riding, calf-riding, sheep-riding contest itself?

The next morning, as I prayed the morning office, I said to God, "Okay. Last night was certainly a new and very different experience for me. But what is the lesson you want me to learn from it?" As I sat in silence, it struck me that no matter where I find myself in this world, no matter who is in front of me, no matter who is behind me, no matter who is to my left, no matter who is to my right, no matter if no one is near, and no matter how strange, or different, or idiosyncratic a situation may be, God is with me. I can, therefore, never be out-of-place. For, if one's eyes are open to see God, if one's ears are open to hear God, if one's heart is open to experience God, then one cannot be out-of-place, but rather, only "in-place," in the deepest sense, because God is near.

Looking out at the cloudless cerulean Arizona sky that morning, I recalled these words, this prayer, of David, son of Jesse, and by God's anointing, king of Israel, a man of dramatic contrasts.

> LORD, you have probed me, you know me: you know when I sit and stand; you understand my thoughts from afar. You sift through my travels and my rest; with all my ways you are familiar. Even before a word is on my tongue, LORD, you know it all.
>
> Behind and before you encircle me and rest your hand upon me. Such knowledge is too wonderful for me, far too lofty for me to reach. Where can I go from your spirit? From your presence, where can I flee? If I ascend to the heavens, you are there; if I lie down in Sheol, there you are. If I take the wings of dawn and dwell beyond the sea, Even there your hand guides me, your right hand holds me fast. (Psalm 139)

Questions:

What about you?

Have you ever felt out-of-place?

Do you pause each and every day to know that God encircles you in love always?

Prayer:

Dear God, sometimes I feel amused, sometimes I feel scared, and sometimes I feel out-of-place. Like your servant David, help me to remember that you know me better than I know myself; with all my ways you are familiar. I pray that by your Grace, no matter where I am, or with whom I am, my eyes and ears and heart are ever more open to see, hear, and experience your enduring and encircling love for me, for others, and for all creation.

FOUR

Shamus

In the summer of 2015, I and seven friends had the good fortune to travel to Ireland to play golf. The eight of us flew out of JFK in New York in the evening of Saturday, July 11, and arrived at Shannon Airport in the early hours of Sunday, July 12. Our first two nights were spent in County Clare, in the seaside town of Lahinch where we stayed at the Lehinch Lodge. With this as our home away from home, we played the historic Lahinch Golf Club (founded in 1892), as well as at the equally stunning oceanside course, Doonbeg.

On day three, we departed from Lahnich, stopped at the Cliffs of Moher only to be confronted by fog so thick that you could hardly see well enough to walk, and made our way down to County Kerry, to the beautiful town of Killarney, where we stayed at the Malton Hotel. With this as our second home away from home, we played three more great golf courses: Ballybunion, Waterville, and Tralee.

On the last night of the trip, three of us had reservations to eat at Bricin, a superb restaurant owned by the McGuire brothers, Johnny and Paddy. Arriving at the restaurant a bit early, Johnny greeted us and told us that our table was not quite ready. Though he would love for us "to take a drink" (as the Irish say) at his restaurant's bar, his liquor license does not permit it; it only allows him to serve drinks to patrons who are seated and eating. Without missing a beat, Johnny encouraged us to go across the street "to take a drink" at a pub named O'Shea's.

To Johnny, I replied, "Why O'Shea's?"

Johnny responded, "You'll see." Directed by our host, off to O'Shea's we went.

Standing on High Street and looking at O'Shea's, it was obvious that O'Shea's was much, much less upscale than Bricin. I thought to myself, *Why this pub? There are so many pubs in Killarney; there are so many pubs right on this street, High Street. Why O'Shea's?* At that moment, one of my friends opened the door and said, "Okay, let's go in and 'take a drink!'" I went in first. The doorway did not lead directly into the pub. It led down a dimly lit and foul-smelling hallway, at the end of which was the doorway into the pub. Gagging for a second or two, I made my way down the hallway only to be startled by a man, quite unkempt, sitting on a stool, himself one source of the awful smell, with a pint of Guinness in one hand and an unlit cigarette in the other. When we made eye contact, he greeted me with these words, "Welcome to O'Shea's, lads. The pub is through this door." Careful not to touch this "vagrant," I made my way into the pub and over to the small bar behind which was the lovely owner, Joan O'Shea. "Welcome, lads!"

she said. "What will you be taking for drink? Guinness? Whiskey?" Having had my fill of Guinness for the trip, and knowing that we were about to have a wonderful dinner at Bricin complemented by good wine, I and my two golfing buddies decided to take a Jameson. Joan set up the three glasses and poured the Jameson. When she handed me my glass, I could not help but notice how unclean it was. *Why? I said to myself. Why did Johnny send us to this place? It smells. It's dirty! Why?* My friends laughed when they saw me eyeing the glass and assured me that the alcohol content of the Jameson was enough to kill any germs that were living in my glass. Laugh, I did not. However, I did take my first sip from the glass.

At that moment, the vagrant who had been sitting in the hallway made his way to the bar and took a seat. Without a word spoken, Joan poured him another Guinness. Then Joan turned to us and said, "I know that you lads have met Shamus already. However, I am guessing that there were no proper introductions. Turning to Shamus, Joan said, "Shamus meet ..." Caught off guard, for sure, as Joan looked right at me, I extended my hand and said my name, "Hi. I'm Ken." My two friends introduced themselves as well. Now, having been properly introduced by Joan, she and Shamus began to tell us Shamus's story. And though he appeared to be no more than a smelly, unshaven drunkard, in point of fact, he was well educated, and if you listened carefully, well spoken. In addition, we learned that Shamus is from one of Killarney's prominent families. Then it hit me. This is why Johnny sent us to O'Shea's "to take a drink." Johnny did not want us to leave Killarney having only been in its finer restaurants, shops, and hotels. Johnny wanted us, typical American tourists, to meet, if you will, the salt of the earth men and women of Ireland: the Joans and Shamuses.

My friends and I were so taken with Shamus and Joan that, following dinner, when we got back to the hotel, we encouraged our other five friends to join us in going back to O'Shea's to meet Joan and Shamus. And so we did. We walked back to O'Shea's and saw Joan, Shamus, and Joan's husband and son as well. We stayed quite awhile enjoying their company and hospitality. The O'Sheas were so proud to open the first floor of their home to old and new friends, and to tell us that they were among only fifteen families in Ireland that owned a pub with a five-generation history of ownership.

On my flight back to the United States, in my private conversation with God, I said, "Okay, God. So this trip wasn't really about the golf, was it? No. It was about you wanting me to meet Shamus and learn, once again, the lesson of seeing, not as we so often see, but of seeing as you see, of seeing in the way you shared with the prophet Samuel: 'Do not judge from ... appearance ... God does not see as a mortal, who sees the appearance. The LORD looks into the heart.'" (1 Samuel 16:7)

Questions:

What about you?

When you see another Shamus, do you avert your eyes or perhaps cross the street? Do you see only his/her appearance, or are you able to see him/her as God does? Are you able to look into his/her heart and be moved knowing that he/she reveals God's presence too?

Prayer:

God of clear vision, as you once opened the eyes of Samuel to see deeply into the mystery of life and love, so, we pray, open our hearts to perceive deeply into the mystery of your presence among us, most especially in the Shamuses of our world. It was so easy, O God, to get stuck in the glamour of the superficial. Inspire us to be more fascinated with the depths of things than to be allured by that which passes so quickly. Amen.

FIVE

Haiti
A Knock at My Window

In the aftermath of the devastating 2010 earthquake in Haiti, I am proud to write that Siena College, my alma mater, a special place where I have lived and worked for nearly twenty years, accepted three Haitian students, gratis, to complete their college/university studies. Two Siena professors (husband/wife), welcomed the three Haitians into their home, and the college welcomed them into the academic community as full-time students. Upon completing their studies, one of the three, Pierre Louis, went back to his homeland to found St. Gabriel's School in

Fontaine. The second, Cenat, went back to Haiti to found St. Francis Xavier Haitian Orphanage in Petite Riviere. Ever since this school and this orphanage have gotten off the ground, on January breaks or spring breaks, Siena College students have traveled to Haiti to volunteer.

In the spring of 2015, I was teaching a seminar entitled "Franciscan Service." This course is part 1 of a two-part course offering. The second course is entitled "Internship in Franciscan Service." The part 1 course provides students with the "intellectual tools," if you will, to understand what Franciscan service is and why it is integral to the mission and identity of Siena College. Having completed this seminar, students are well equipped to go forth and serve, but this time with the ability to make meaning from their experience from a Roman Catholic and Franciscan point of view, hence, the second course. In the "Internship in Franciscan Service" course, for academic credit, students serve locally, nationally, and internationally and reflect upon their service, making use of what they learned in the first course.

As the spring 2015 unfolded, I thought to myself what a great idea it would be for me and future seminar students to go and serve somewhere together and to reflect upon our work together. Thus, in the summer of 2015, I began a conversation with some folks who serve on the board for St. Francis Xavier Haitian Orphanage Foundation. I knew that several of the board members had traveled to the orphanage. I shared with them that I would like to take Siena students there, either in January 2016 or spring break 2016. We agreed that it would be best for me to travel with board members first to get a feel for the place and then think about bringing students at some future date.

So, on January 7, 2016, I, along with five other adults from St. Pius X Parish (three of whom are board members), Loudonville, New York, left for Haiti. We arrived in Port-au-Prince just before noon. The airport was crowded and hot. To get all of our luggage (we each brought an extra bag filled with supplies for the orphanage and gifts for the children) and to get to the van was not easy. There were so many Haitians wanting to assist us in any way so as to receive a tip. With the assistance of Cenat; our Haitian driver, Jack; and a police officer from Petite Riviere who was hired to be with us for our entire time on the island, we eventually loaded the van and pickup truck and made our way out of the airport and into the streets of Port-au-Prince.

I was immediately struck by the amount of traffic and the number of people. Even more so, I was struck by the amount of garbage that littered the streets. After a quick lunch and cold beer, Haiti's own *Prestige* lager beer, we made our way to a dental clinic in Port-au-Prince that takes care of the children in the orphanage.

Late that afternoon, we headed north for what would be a three-hour drive to Petite Riviere. Along the way, we made a few stops to pick up supplies. The last stop we made was in St. Mark, a town of almost seventy thousand people. St. Mark is approximately thirty minutes from Petite Riviere. While Cenat went into a store to buy blocks of ice (the orphanage has no refrigeration), we, the six white Americans and our Haitian driver, sat in the van parked on what appeared to be a town square and waited. We must have waited at least fifteen minutes, and with each passing minute, I became more and more uncomfortable with the number of Haitians who were peering into the van and begging. Sitting in the second row of seats next to the window, it was not easy for me to avoid eye contact.

Startled by a knock at my window, I turned and saw a Haitian woman, probably in her early twenties, pregnant, and, in one arm, and resting on one hip, was a young boy, presumably her son. We made eye contact ever so briefly, and then I turned away. *Where is Cenat?* I said to myself. *Let's get out of here!* I thought. And as my sense of discomfort moved into fear, there was a second knock at the window. I looked again. Then, ever so slowly, this young woman pointed to me, then pointed to the boy on her hip, then to her child in her womb, then to herself, and then up to the heavens, as if to say: "Hey, God sees you, and you see me and my two kids, so please help us." At that moment, though it was nearly ninety degrees out, I felt a chill run down my spine. I looked away again. Cenat finally came, and we sped off to Petite Riviere. The experience haunted me for the entire time I was in Haiti. It still haunts me. God did see me in that moment. God does see me in each moment of my life. And God the Father is always calling me to be like God's Son, Christ Jesus, not turning away from human suffering, but rather stepping into it, responding to it selflessly and generously with mercy.

Months after this experience, when Luke's "Feeding of the Five Thousand" was the Sunday Gospel, for some reason, I read it with new eyes, heard it with new ears, and felt it with a new heart.

> When the apostles returned, they explained to him what they had done. He took them and withdrew in private to a town called Bethsaida. The crowds, meanwhile, learned of this and followed him. He received them and spoke to them about the kingdom of God, and he healed those who needed to be cured. As the day was drawing to a close, the Twelve approached him and said, "Dismiss the crowd so that they can go to the surrounding villages and farms and find lodging and provisions; for we are in a deserted place here." He said to them, "Give them some food yourselves." They replied, "Five loaves and two fish are all we have, unless we ourselves

go and buy food for all these people." Now the men there numbered about five thousand. Then he said to his disciples, "Have them sit down in groups of [about] fifty." They did so and made them all sit down. Then taking the five loaves and the two fish, and looking up to heaven, he said the blessing over them, broke them, and gave them to the disciples to set before the crowd. They all ate and were satisfied. And when the leftover fragments were picked up, they filled twelve wicker baskets. (LK 9:10–17)

Questions:

What about you?

For reasons of discomfort or fear, have you turned away from human suffering?

However few the fish, however small the loaf of bread you may have, what can you do, what will you do this day to "step into" human suffering with love?

Prayer:

Lord Jesus, you entered into the chaos of our world to set us free from fear. Strengthen me, so that beyond my fears, I may be most willing to enter into the chaos of others. As you asked your disciples to bring to you what few resources they had, fish and bread, now I offer you my humble resources and ask you to multiply them so that I will not be so afraid or hesitant to share them with anyone who knocks at the window of my life.

SIX

The Gift of Compassion

It was the fall of 1977. My older sister, Lucia, was beginning her first year at Rhode Island College, RIC for short, in Providence, Rhode Island. I was beginning my last year, my senior year, at John F. Kennedy Catholic High School, a private Roman Catholic high school in the Archdiocese of New York. Kennedy was founded by and is staffed by the Sisters of Divine Compassion. My younger sister, Lia, was beginning her first year of high school at John Jay High School, the local public high school.

Like many seniors in high school, I was focused on finishing well my high school career and getting into the college of my choice. At this point, my dad, in his midforties, had been a partner in a family business, Albano Appliance and Electric, for nearly twenty years. This is a major appliance business as well as a residential electrical contracting business established by my maternal grandparents in Pound Ridge, New York. At the time, my father and my two uncles (my mom's brothers) were the three partners.

Though my father felt fine, I remember him going to our family physician, Dr. Pappalardo, in Bedford, New York, because he was concerned about some blood in his stool. Our doc sent him immediately to Northern Westchester Hospital, and, literally, the next day, he was operated on for colorectal cancer. The colostomy was irreversible. My mom sat my sisters and me down and shared the difficult news that my father had cancer. Moreover, the docs hoped that the surgery had gotten everything, which is to say, that the cancer had not already spread to some other part of my dad's body. Cancer? An aggressive cancer? How could this be? My father had just turned forty-five, and only a few months ago!

With a lump in my throat, a knot in my stomach, and tears in my eyes, my mom, my sisters, and I walked through the door of my father's hospital room. I remember clearly seeing so many tubes, IVs and monitors attached to my dad as he struggled to recover from major surgery. Though conscious, he could not speak and was too weak even to hold our hands. It was shocking to see a man who once was so healthy, so strong, now appear so ill, so weak. I just could not believe that this was happening to him. I just could not believe that this was happening to my mom and my sisters. I just could not believe that this was happening to me.

In the weeks that followed his surgery, I worked ever harder in school and in my after-school job in the family business. I had little interest in talking to anyone about my father's state of health. I just wanted him to recover completely and for things to return to the way they were before cancer had visited him and my family.

Later that fall, while at Kennedy, I remember the bell ringing, signaling the end of senior religion class with Sr. Dolores Mascalli, RDC, a member of the Sisters of Divine Compassion. As I gathered my belongings and headed to the door, Sr. Dolores stopped me and asked me to come to her office for a minute. "Sure," I said. She invited me to take a seat, which I did. She sat across from me. And looking me in the eyes, she said, "I know about your dad. How is he? How are you?" And in that very tender moment, having kept so much inside for so long, I burst into tears and let myself be hugged by this nun, this sister of Divine Compassion and Love. I did not say much that day but knew that this experience of compassion would allow me to be more open to talking to Sr. Dolores if and when I needed to do so. She played an important role in my senior year of high school. In fact, she played an important role in the lifelong project of welcoming the Lord's compassion into my life, so that I, in turn, can give away what I have been freely given—Divine Compassion.

At seventeen years of age, I knew enough to know that indeed God's life was shared with me through Sr. Dolores's embrace. And ever since that day, I say to God, "Help me to see and be open to the Sr. Dolores whom you choose each day to lift me up." In other words, over time, my prayer has become one of trusting that God does reveal God's compassion to me each day, often in and through the most unlikely of candidates.

Recall Mary's trip to and visit with her cousin Elizabeth found in the first chapter of Luke's Gospel:

> During those days Mary set out and traveled to the hill country in haste to a town of Judah, where she entered the house of Zechariah and greeted Elizabeth. When Elizabeth heard Mary's greeting, the infant leaped in her womb, and Elizabeth, filled with the holy Spirit, cried out in a loud voice and said, "Most blessed are you among women, and blessed is the fruit of your womb. And how does this happen to me, that the mother of my Lord should come to me? For at the moment the sound of your greeting reached my ears, the infant in my womb leaped for joy. Blessed are you who believed that what was spoken to you by the Lord would be fulfilled."

And Mary said: "My soul proclaims the greatness of the Lord; my spirit rejoices in God my savior. For he has looked upon his handmaid's lowliness; behold, from now on will all ages call me blessed. The Mighty One has done great things for me, and holy is his name. His mercy is from age to age to those who fear him. He has shown might with his arm, dispersed the arrogant of mind and heart. He has thrown down the rulers from their thrones but lifted up the lowly. The hungry he has filled with good things; the rich he has sent away empty. He has helped Israel his servant, remembering his mercy, according to his promise to our fathers, to Abraham and to his descendants forever." Mary remained with her about three months and then returned to her home. (LK 1:39–56)

Questions:

What about you?

Will you allow God to embrace you this day with God's mantle of compassion?

Like Mary did for Elizabeth and Elizabeth did for Mary, will you, in turn, share that embrace with another, especially one who is afraid or alone?

Prayer:

Dear Mary, Mother of God, as you and Elizabeth found consolation in each other, and as I was consoled by the visitation and embrace of my teacher, so dear Mother of God, wrap your mantle around those who are afraid and alone, those who are surprised with unexpected news, so that in the midst of all the impermanence of living, we may find a sure refuge in your visitation to us, O Clement, O Loving, O Sweet Virgin Mary.

SEVEN

Weston Priory

As a follower of St. Francis of Assisi, as a Franciscan priest, I am a member of the *Ordo Fratrum Minorum*, the Order of Friars Minor, the Order of Lesser Brothers. I took my Solemn Vows, or Final Vows of Poverty, Chastity, and Obedience on June 17, 1989. The then minister general of the order, an American from California, Fr. John Vaughn, OFM, was the one who received my vows, as he was on Siena College's campus for a fraternal gathering of my province, the Province of the Most Holy Name of Jesus, New York City.

Prior to that amazing day, my Solemn Profession classmates and I had to make a three-week retreat. For the first two weeks, we retreated together in what once was our Retreat Center in Rye Beach, New Hampshire. For the third and final week, each of us had to choose a place in which we would make a seven-day silent retreat. I chose Weston Priory in Weston, Vermont. Inspired by a monastic tradition reaching back to the earliest centuries of the church and shaped by the Rule of Saint Benedict, founded in 1953, the Weston Priory monks' life together centers on prayer, manual work, and hospitality to retreatants like me.

Alone, I stayed in a guest house completely separate from the monks' residence. My classmates and I were instructed not to bring any reading materials other than our Sacred Scriptures and the writings of St. Francis and St. Clare of Assisi. I did share in the common meals and prayers of the monks. The only words spoken or heard were at prayer and the Table Reading that took place during the common meals. Even if I had wanted to, there was no television, no

62

computer, no smart phone. There was simply the beauty of the Weston Priory grounds and silence.

Though I knew that St. Francis of Assisi was *not* a monk, I also knew that he spent a good amount of time alone and in prayer. I dreaded this week. My life is far more active than it is contemplative. Why did my province insist that we make this silent retreat when, in fact, we are a very active province?

Day one of my silent retreat was okay because it was all new to me. Even day two was okay. The weather was beautiful. The monks' prayer life was rich. The food they generously shared was simple and delicious. Day three, however, did not go so well. In fact, I was tempted to get in my car and drive to anyplace where I could see and talk to someone. It did not matter to me if that seeing/hearing took place in a restaurant, supermarket, pharmacy, gas station, or mall. I just wanted to break the silence. And then I remembered the story of Elijah and how he, though difficult, had to learn to find God in the silence.

In the First Book of Kings, recall how Jezebel murdered all the prophets except Elijah. In response, Elijah fled from her and sought refuge in the wilderness. It was there that he came to a solitary broom tree and sat beneath it. There Elijah prayed for death saying:

> "Enough, LORD! Take my life, for I am no better than my ancestors." He lay down and fell asleep under the solitary broom tree, but suddenly a messenger touched him and said, "Get up and eat!" He looked and there at his head was a hearth cake and a jug of water. After he ate and drank, he lay down again, but the angel of the LORD came back a second time, touched him, and said, "Get up and eat or the journey will be too much for you!" He got up, ate, and drank; then strengthened by that food, he walked forty days and forty nights to the mountain of God, Horeb.
>
> There he came to a cave, where he took shelter. But the word of the LORD came to him: "Why are you here, Elijah?" He answered: "I have been most zealous for the LORD, the God of hosts, but the Israelites have forsaken your covenant. They have destroyed your altars and murdered your prophets by the sword. I alone remain, and they seek to take my life." Then the LORD said: "Go out and stand on the mountain before the LORD; the LORD will pass by." There was a strong and violent wind rending the mountains and crushing rocks before the LORD—but the LORD was not in the wind; after

the wind, an earthquake—but the LORD was not in the earthquake; after the earthquake, fire—but the LORD was not in the fire; after the fire, a light silent sound. When he heard this, Elijah hid his face in his cloak and went out and stood at the entrance of the cave. (1KG 19:4–13)

It is not that God could not have revealed God's self in and through the strong wind. It is not that God could not have revealed God's self in and through the earthquake. It is not that God could not have revealed God's self in and through the fire. Rather, it is that God chose to reveal God's self in and through the *silence*, and only those whose hearts and ears are listening can come to know God's presence in and through the silence.

I prayed over this text for the remaining days of my "silent retreat." And indeed I came to hear and experience God ever more powerfully in the "light silent sound" of Weston, Vermont.

That week was nearly thirty years ago. And do you want to know something? I have never made a "silent retreat" since then. However, ever since that week in 1989, amidst what have been more than thirty years of serving God's people in active ministry, I do my best, each day, to be quiet, to be still, at least for a few minutes. In and through those moments of silence, however brief, I pray for the Grace to see, to hear, to respond to the God who reveals God's self in countless ways, including silence.

The funny thing is that as I have gotten older (especially these past twenty years), as I have lived in a larger friary of nearly thirty of my brothers, especially as I continue to work on a very busy college campus, especially as I preach and preside at many places in the Albany Diocese, I have come to appreciate that, in fact, I need alone time each day when I return to my room, my cell, my sanctuary. For it is within these four walls, my room, my home, that, in silence, I thank God for showing me God's face in all that has been my life that day—especially in and through the moments of silence.

Questions:

What about you?

Is silence something you seek or avoid in life?

When you are silent, no matter how infrequently or how briefly, what do you hear in and through the silence?

Prayer:

Dear God of Elijah and all the prophets, reveal yourself to us again and again in the unexpected silences that punctuate our lives and which so often we are afraid to enter. Strengthen us and give us courage to enter these silent moments. Help us to realize that in and through them, the profound song of your presence can shake our hearts and set us free.

EIGHT

EIGHT

East Side Elementary School

My niece, Caitlin, is a special education teacher at East Side Elementary School, Chattanooga, Tennessee. For the academic year 2012–13, this was the profile for the K-5 school:

553 students

33% African American

.2% Asian

60.9% Hispanic

.2% Native American

5.8% White

95+% "Economically Disadvantaged"

47.2% Female

52.8% Male

In Caitlin's first year at East Side, academic year 2014–15, my niece shared with me the following story. As a new teacher in the building, she was certainly interested in getting to know her students and, in ways appropriate, for her students to get to know her. With the summer heat of mid-August, in those first few days of "getting to know each other," Caitlin said to her students that they could ask her a few questions. And so her students did. The conversation went something like this:

"Ms. Hill, you got any kids?"

"No. I do not have any kids."

"Ms. Hill, you got a man?"

"No. I do not have a man."

"Ms. Hill, if you ain't got any kids, and you ain't got a man … then what you got?"

Chuckling to herself, Caitlin responded, "I have a dog and two cats." Her students responded with blank stares, open mouths, and no words.

Notice the order of questions. The first question was in regards to children. The second question had to do with a husband, I assume. Given the responses of no and no, think about the students' final comment: "If you ain't got kids, and you ain't got a man ... then what you got?" From their point of view, from their world, no kids and no man means, as a young woman, that you quite literally have nothing in this life.

Upon hearing my niece tell this story, my first response was to laugh; it is a funny story. However, the more I thought about it, on another level, it was curious that this particular class of students, young boys and girls who come from families and homes that are economically disadvantaged (a euphemism for poor), do not think that a young woman, a teacher, a professional, can have anything in life if she does not have kids or a man.

In my niece's second year at East Side, I had the opportunity to visit her, her students, and the larger East Side School community. On that day in May, a school-wide, all-day, outdoor Field Day, I met her principal. I met her assistant principal. I met her K-3 special education teaching partner. Most important, I met several of her students, most of whom were current students of hers, but some were former students. Of the students whom I met, almost all have names with which I was unfamiliar. I met Damoney, Zitorie, Yaneli, Vividiana, Chioke, Chittarius, Nyterrius, Mycurious, and Keshaunti. And interestingly, though these students are all students of color, though many were learning English as a second language, though all were from "poor" families/homes, though they thought that my niece "ain't got nothing" because she is not married and does not have children, it struck me that these kids, my niece's students, are kids much like any other school's kids are kids. They hugged me. They wanted me to play games with them. They were curious about me. When they heard that I was from New York, they assumed that meant New York City, and they wanted to know if I knew Donald Trump! In other words, I began to realize that underneath all of their social conditioning and expectations, underneath their unique names, underneath their socioeconomic status, underneath their struggles to learn and communicate in a new language, they are children like any other children.

I chuckled to myself and began to pray: "Oh yes, God, you knew what you were doing when you created humanity. You know what you are doing when you create each human being uniquely. O God, indeed, each one of us is a wonder of your making, a wonder of your hands, a wonder of your glorious image and likeness."

That night I reread the first creation story from the book of Genesis. In particular, I was drawn to day six:

> Then God said: Let us make human beings in our image, after our likeness. Let them have dominion over the fish of the sea, the birds of the air, the tame animals, all the wild animals, and all the creatures that crawl on the earth.
>
> God created mankind in his image; in the image of God he created them; male and female he created them. God blessed them and God said to them: Be fertile and multiply; fill the earth and subdue it. Have dominion over the fish of the sea, the birds of the air, and all the living things that crawl on the earth.

God also said: See, I give you every seed-bearing plant on all the earth and every tree that has seed-bearing fruit on it to be your food; and to all the wild animals, all the birds of the air, and all the living creatures that crawl on the earth, I give all the green plants for food. And so it happened. God looked at everything he had made, and found it *very good* [italics added]. Evening came, and morning followed—the sixth day. (GN 1:26–31)

Questions:

What about you?

Do you see yourself as a wonder of God's hands, God's creation?

Consider the person you like least. Can you see him/her also as a wonder of God's hands?

When you look out at humanity, do you see that underneath the countless differences that manifest themselves across this planet, there is a common thread running through us all—we are the image and likeness of God?

Prayer:

Dear God of the *Very Good*, you have given us all that we need to delight in your immense creation. Like little children, help us to be curious about the mysteries of life so that we may reach out to each other in joy and enjoy each other's company with you, the source of all goodness and life.

NINE

Haiti
No Shoes

The second to last day of our mission to Haiti was on Sunday, January 10, 2016. It was the Feast of the Baptism of the Lord. Naturally, we gathered for Sunday Mass. What was particularly significant, however, was that at that Mass we would also celebrate sixteen Baptisms and fifteen first Holy Communions of many children at the orphanage. In the Haitian Catholic culture, first Holy Communion is a "big deal," even for those children who come from families with very little. Somehow, families, church communities, and town folk manage to find the resources to make sure those about to be baptized and those about to receive Holy Communion are dressed beautifully. Somehow, those who surround these little ones, in love, do what they need to do in order to have a great party following the celebration.

I remember so clearly getting up early that morning (I never slept well on that trip!) and helping set up more than two-hundred-fifty chairs, for the whole town of Petite Riviere had been invited to this special Mass. Almost two hours before the Mass was to begin, as we continued to set up for this special occasion, I saw an elderly Haitian man walking up the driveway. He surveyed our work to figure out where he wanted to sit. He was dressed in a suit, yes, but a very old and tattered one. He did have on a shirt and tie, yes, but the shirt was hardly recognizable as a white shirt since it was so stained and dirty. What most caught my attention, however, was the fact that he wore no shoes; his feet were bare, swollen, bruised, and, honestly, filthy. Here he was, an elderly man dressed in a threadbare suit, walking barefoot for who knows how far, to celebrate Mass with these orphaned children. I was humbled. He took a seat toward the front and said his prayers as we continued to set up for the Mass.

Many times during the Mass, as I looked out at the those assembled to hear God's Word and receive the Bread of Life and the Cup of Salvation, I was struck by the contrast between the pristine white dresses and white suits on the girls and boys respectively, and the tired, decrepit, and dirty suit on the old man. In terms of apparel, the differences could not be more evident.

For as many Masses, Baptisms, and first Holy Communions that I have presided over or attended in my North American culture, I have never been to one where anyone came wearing dirty old clothes and no shoes. Equally evident, and even more powerful, however, was the fact that *all*, regardless of attire, regardless of age, regardless of gender, were gathered around the One Table to receive the One Bread and the One Cup. The children, the old man, and all the rest of us came to receive a gift, the gift of gifts, Jesus Christ.

At that moment, it struck me anew: in baptism, in terms of earthly clothes, regardless of what we are wearing or not, we are clothed in Christ and become new creations. And when the baptized gather as a Eucharistic community, we are grateful for the gift that we are and are becoming, that is, God's chosen ones holy and beloved. We are grateful to live no longer in our narrow identities but rather as a people through whom Christ lives.

Here I am reminded of what the apostle Paul wrote to the early Christian community in Galatia:

> For through the law I died to the law, that I might live for God. I have been crucified with Christ; yet I live, no longer I, but Christ lives in me; insofar as I now live in the flesh, I live by faith in the Son of God who has loved me and given himself up for me. (GA 2:19–20)

St. Paul, apostle to the Gentiles, continued with these words:

> For through faith you are all children of God in Christ Jesus. For all of you who were baptized into Christ have clothed yourselves with Christ. There is neither Jew nor Greek, there is neither slave nor free person, there is not male and female; for you are all

one in Christ Jesus. And if you belong to Christ, then you are Abraham's descendant, heirs according to the promise. (GA 3:26–29)

As we flew back to the United States, for sure I was eager to take a long, hot shower. For sure I was eager to eat something other than rice and beans. For sure I was eager to have ready access to clean drinking water. I was also eager, however, to begin again; to live life grateful for so much, but especially for being clothed in Christ and the dignity therein regardless of our earthly attire.

Questions:

And what about you?

Is it enough for you to know that you have been clothed in Christ and are now a new creation?

What did the old man know/feel that you may not?

Prayer:

O God of the Great Promise, you have given us the hope that one day we will be clothed in glory. Already clothed in Christ through Baptism, help us to see with your eyes and to recognize Christ in others no matter how they are clothed, no matter whether they wear shoes or not. Help us to remember that Jesus died naked on Calvary's cross in front of his own mother. Help us to remember that by his nakedness, every human being is clothed with dignity. Like Paul, may this remembrance of dignity move us to live lives of faith most especially on behalf of the poorest among us.

TEN

TEN

Home
and
Yet so Far from Home

All of the stories I have shared in the preceding chapters took place in settings other than my home. Some took place in other countries: Ireland and Haiti. Others took place in other states within these United States: Arizona, Vermont, and Tennessee. And still others took place in cities or towns within New York State other than my hometown, Troy and Somers. This final chapter, however, centers upon my life at home; that is to say, my life as a Franciscan priest who lives and works at Siena College in Loudonville, New York. In the following pages, I wish to underscore the point that one does not need to travel outside the walls of one's home to encounter God in that which is new, or different, or unfamiliar, or unknown. No—our omnipresent God quite often reveals God's self in the expected and unexpected moments of life at home. Allow me to share a final story.

At the end of a recent academic year, once again, my work at the college changed. To transition from full-time administration back to full-time teaching, I took a long overdue sabbatical with the purpose of writing this book. In the previous chapters, I shared personal stories of encountering God outside the walls of my home and outside the walls of my daily life. As the writing got under way, however, I was reminded that one need not leave home in order to ask and grapple with some of life's more important questions. The more I wrote, the more I thought about life beyond my one-year sabbatical. As an American male in my fifties, as one who was at the same academic institution for nearly twenty years, I began to wonder: *Should I pursue academic leadership at another institution? Should I return to the faculty with my tenure? Should I do something totally different in terms of work, perhaps parish ministry or parish mission ministry?* Typical for me, I talked to trusted friends and colleagues. Moreover, I brought my questions to God in prayer.

As I struggled to do less talking in prayer and more listening, I began to realize God's response was quite different from what I expected. I recalled the quip: "If you want to hear God laugh, tell God your plans!" Though God surely heard my three questions (see above), after all, God is omniscient, God chose not to answer the questions as I had posed them. God did not say, "Yes, pursue an academic leadership position at another institution." God did not say, "Yes, go back to the faculty as a tenured associate professor." God did not say, "Yes, go and work in a completely different setting such as a parish." Rather, and quite challenging, deep within, I heard God say, "Trust Me." "Trust Me?" What kind of response is that to my questions? "Please, God," I replied, "I need to know what I should do professionally." As I sat in silence, as I breathed more slowly and deeply, as I listened even more closely, God spoke again:

"Yes, I have heard your good questions, but listen to my response; it has nothing to do with place or type of work; it has to do with your faith in Me. Know that wherever you are in the world, know that whatever you are doing, if you trust in Me, you will be embraced more deeply by My love, and you will be opened to a peace that you never imagined possible because you trust in Me. That's what really matters. The rest are just details. I gave you a brain. You figure it out. Trust Me. Trust Me. Trust Me."

Moved to tears, I continued to pray in silence. After what seemed like an hour, but more likely was a few minutes, God continued to respond to me with a few questions of God's own!

"Do you, will you, trust Me in the midst of change and disruption?"

"Is your faith strong enough to trust in My abiding presence?"

"Am I the center of your life?"

"Do you, will you, seek first the kingdom of Heaven?"

"Are you willing to let go and stop holding on?"

"Do you know that you are not in control?"

"With joy, will you say yes to my larger project, design, plan for you?"

As I heard these questions, I continued to cry knowing the truth and wisdom of God's questions for me. That night, I dreamed of Abraham (Abram) and Sarah (Sarai) leaving their home, trusting themselves to the promise of God. Read these words anew:

> The LORD said to Abram: Go forth from your land, your relatives, and from your father's house to a land that I will show you. I will make of you a great nation, and I will bless you; I will make your name great, so that you will be a blessing. I will bless those who bless you and curse those who curse you. All the families of the earth will find blessing in you. Abram went as the LORD directed him, and Lot went with him. Abram was seventy-five years old when he left Haran. Abram took his wife Sarai, his brother's son

Lot, all the possessions that they had accumulated, and the persons they had acquired in Haran, and they set out for the land of Canaan. When they came to the land of Canaan, Abram passed through the land as far as the sacred place at Shechem, by the oak of Moreh. The Canaanites were then in the land. The LORD appeared to Abram and said: To your descendants I will give this land. So Abram built an altar there to the LORD who had appeared to him. From there he moved on to the hill country east of Bethel, pitching his tent with Bethel to the west and Ai to the east. He built an altar there to the LORD and invoked the LORD by name. (GN 12:1–8)

Questions:

What about you?

In prayer, are you more of a talker or more of a listener?

When you listen in prayer, what do you hear? Are you surprised by what God has to say to you?

In the ordinary moments of your daily life, your life at home, your life at work, do you see God? Do you hear God? Do you "feel" God?

Like Abraham and Sarah, whether you are "at home," or you are "far from home," are you willing to be led by God not knowing where the path goes?

And on that path, when you experience life's chaos, do you trust in God's abiding presence and love for you?

Prayer:

My God, my God, why have you forsaken me? Know, dear Lord, that sometimes I feel like praying these words, words that your only Son spoke from the cross. And then, dear

God, as you did with your only Son, you speak to me and remind me that you are with us always even until the end of time. And then I pray something different. I say: "Open my ears that I may hear. Open my eyes that I might see. Open my heart that I may receive the Good News of your presence and promise. Amen."

About the Author

Fr. Paulli, a Franciscan priest of Holy Name Province for nearly thirty years, is a member of the First Year Seminar faculty, as well as an associate professor of education at Siena College, Loudonville, New York.

He is a popular speaker at conferences, retreats, and parish missions across the United States.

Fr. Paulli holds a bachelor's degree in business from Siena College, a master's degree in systematic theology from the Washington Theological Union, and a doctorate in religion and education from New York City's Columbia University.

Outside the Walls: Encountering God in the Unfamiliar is Fr. Paulli's first published book.

About the Artist

Alan Colavecchio is a graphic designer, illustrator and painter. He has a marketing and advertising business in Winsted, Connecticut.

Printed in the United States
By Bookmasters